Charisma

The Best Tactics to Be More Charismatic, Likable, and to Impress Anyone

Table of Contents

Introduction	5
Chapter 1: The Art and Science of Charisma and Why Is It Important?	7
Chapter 2: The Mind	10
Chapter 3: The Body	31
Chapter 4: The Relationship	38
Chapter 5: Putting It All Together	48
Conclusion	52

© Copyright 2017 by Cameron Laws - All rights reserved.

The following eBook is reproduced below with the goal of providing information that is as accurate and reliable as possible. Regardless, purchasing this eBook is consent to the author of this book that any actions taken by the reader is in no way the responsibility of the writer and that any recommendations or suggestions that are made herein are solely for recommendation purposes only.

This declaration is deemed fair and valid by both the American Bar Association and the Committee of Publishers Association and is legally binding throughout the United States.

Furthermore, the transmission, duplication or reproduction of any of the following work including specific information will be considered an illegal act irrespective of if it is done electronically or in print. This extends to creating a secondary or tertiary copy of the work or a recorded copy and is only allowed with the express written consent of the Publisher. All additional right reserved.

The information in the following pages is broadly considered to be a truthful and accurate account of facts and as such, any intentional use or misuse of the information in question by the reader will render any resulting actions solely under their jurisdiction. There are no scenarios in which the publisher or the original author of this work can be in any fashion deemed liable for any hardship or damages that may befall the reader after undertaking information described herein.

Additionally, the information in the following pages is intended only for informational purposes and should thus be thought of as universal. As befitting its nature, it is presented without assurance regarding its prolonged validity or interim quality. Trademarks that are mentioned are done without written consent and can in no way be considered an endorsement from the trademark holder.

Introduction

Congratulations on buying this book and thank you for doing so.

The following chapters will discuss Charisma – what it is, why it's important, and several tips and tricks that will allow you to become charismatic. The thing to remember about charisma is that you are not born with it – it is developed. How it's developed is as varied as the number of charismatic people out there. However, there are some things that many of them have in common. In the chapters that follow you will learn just how you can implement strategies and tactics to develop charisma in your life. Just a few of these tips are:

- Improve your attitude
- Be grateful
- Think on your feet
- Know a little about a lot
- Have empathy
- Eye contact
- Mirror

    and so much more...

In this book, you will be given the opportunity to apply proven methods and tips that are known to develop charisma. Make no mistake, developing charisma takes consistent work. Like with anything of value, just doing it once won't help you. Take what you will learn and make it part of your lifestyle. With consistent application, in time, you will start to bring out that charismatic person that's been waiting to come out. The journey you are about to embark on has the ability to change you and the way you view the world.

There are plenty of books on this subject on the market, thanks again for choosing this one! Every effort was made to ensure it is full of as much useful information as possible, please enjoy!

Chapter 1: The Art and Science of Charisma and Why Is It Important?

What is Charisma?

At its core, charisma is being attractive in such a way that others are inspired by you. This is something that is a learned behavior. Charisma starts in early childhood when we are experimenting and finding our way. As children, our life is full of experimentation. We notice things that, as adults, we stop noticing or take for granted. Some of these things we noticed and emulated as children will be covered in throughout this book. According to Olivia Fox Cabane, in her book, *The Charisma Myth: How Anyone Can Master the Art and Science of Personal Magnetism,* charisma is made up of three basic components: presence, power, and warmth. You will discover how to display these three keys in the following chapters and tips. For now, let's look at the Art of Charisma.

The Art

You can liken the Art of Charisma to a dance. If you were to look at a dancer there is a lot of technique and science that go into a performance. However, that isn't what most people go to watch. Fans of dance go to enjoy the art of the dance and to be moved emotionally. It is the combination of the music choice, the lighting, and all the different aspects of dance, like the movement and the facial expressions. When a fan of dance witnesses an amazing performance they are moved through many different emotions. How the steps and the movements are put together, plus the way the dance is expressed, accounts for the art of dance. With charisma, there is a lot of science behind how and why charisma works but at the end of the day, there is a real art to the way it all works. By the end of this book, you will see how the Art of Charisma is effectively implemented.

In the meantime, think about this for a moment. Going back to dance analogy, you may be a fan of different dancers or types of dance, and for different reasons. It doesn't make one better than the other. They have a place in your heart for a reason. The same goes for charisma. Not every charismatic person exudes charisma in the same way; however, they do have some similar tendencies and actions that they take. How they apply these actions is the art.

The Science

Again, going with the dance analogy, the science of dance has some more concrete definitions. First, you have the dance itself. You have a lot of technical things happening within a dance that deals with physics, the anatomy of movement, and Sports science. Then you have the emotional aspects of science. There is the feeling they get when they are watching a dance performance. This feeling or emotion creates chemical releases in the brain and body. This brings chemistry and neuroscience into play. Yes, you can argue that the emotion is the art, but really it is both. How the emotion is conveyed is the art and how the emotion is received and interpreted can be looked at as the science.

So how does dance relate to the art and science of charisma? The many aspects of charisma that you will learn in this book are very much like a dance. Like a dancer, there is preparation you must go through before the actual performance. There is the preparation of the mind and body which leads to your performance in the interactions with others, in other words, your relationships. Let's first take a look at the mind and how you can prepare yourself to be more charismatic.

Chapter 2: The Mind

There is no secret that the mind is extremely powerful. It controls everything we do. It controls the way we act and those actions govern how we perceive our environment and the way we are perceived. So it makes sense that if you are going to learn charisma, you start with your most powerful tool.

Tip #1 - Declutter Your Mind

With so much social media, news, and the fast-paced environment around us, our minds today are more cluttered than in any point in history. With a cluttered mind, 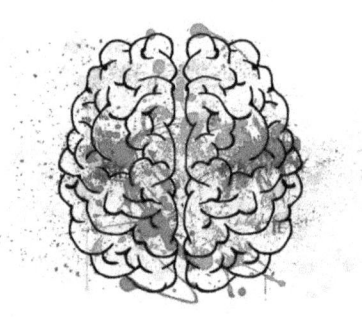 you will miss some of the clues and observations that we will speak about later in the relationships chapter. For now, here are a few ways to help declutter your mind.

1) The first is deep breathing. We will go into this more in the next section but you can incorporate this with meditation.

2) Meditation is a well-known way to clear your mind. Some do this as part of their morning routine while others meditate several times a day. Pick a time that works best for you and incorporate this daily. You will like the results with respect to stress relief and mental clarity.

3) Another thing you can do, which may not seem so obvious, is set goals. Because we have so much going on, our minds are running in different directions. Setting goals is a good way to help you stay focused. When you narrow your focus down to something like a goal you are, by default, neglecting other thoughts that could consume your mind.

4) The last way, and certainly not least, is to simplify. Our lives are so busy and this business often stops people dead in their tracks. See what you can eliminate and take steps to simplify your life.

There are much more ways you can declutter your mind but these first few ways will get you started and I'm sure you will begin to see results. I encourage you to seek more ways to declutter your mind. There is a great book by SJ Scott and Barrie Davenport called *Declutter Your Mind: How to Stop Worrying, Relieve Anxiety, and Eliminate Negative Thinking*. Scott and Davenport outlined several ways for you to gain more mental clarity.

Tip #2 – Breathe

Breathing is the basis for your survival. Without oxygen, you die. However, some of us simply forget to breathe. We either get caught up in what we are doing or we succumb to our stress and don't allow enough oxygen to fill our lungs and supply our brain with the much-needed oxygen. Have you ever noticed that a person with charisma is usually calm? You rarely, if ever, see them stressed out. One of the secrets of charismatic people is that they have learned to control their breathing. Try it for a moment. Take a deep breath in through your nose, hold it for three seconds, and then exhale. Do it again and then again, one more time. Do you feel a difference? Imagine how much different your day would be if you remembered to breathe like this throughout the day. How different would your day be if you were to decrease your stress simply by breathing? Those with a high level of charisma have learned to incorporate deep breathing and breath control as part of their daily routine. They either do this as part of the meditation we spoke about earlier or through exercise. You don't need to do anything elaborate. Just an easy 20-minute walk each day will do the trick. Remember to take the time to breathe and you will notice how different your day becomes.

Tip #3 Write It down

This actually could be a subsection of the declutter your mind tip; however, I think this warrants its own section. Since most of us have so many thoughts swirling around in our head it is impossible to keep track of all of it, even as powerful as our brain is. The simple act of writing something down removes the thought from your brain and helps to declutter your mind. Why does this happen? It is a way of organizing. Think about cleaning out and organizing a garage. The first thing you do is pull everything out of the garage. This allows you to see everything that is there and allows you to put each item back in an organized fashion while, at the same time, allowing you to pick out what needs to be tossed out.

The same holds true with your thoughts. Putting things on paper allows you to pull your thoughts out of your head and put them in a place where you can physically see them. Now I know you can keep track of these thoughts on your phones or laptops, but you can take this to another level. You can do this by going old school and putting pen to paper. Studies have shown that the act of physically writing things down allows you to separate your thoughts because you are using more senses and parts of your body. There is a liberating feeling when you are able to make this separation.

Tip #4 Sleep

Unfortunately, most of us don't get enough sleep. We often hear ourselves and others saying, "there are just not enough hours in the day". Lack of sleep over a long period of time can make it difficult for you to function. While everyone is different, the recommended amount of sleep, as I'm sure you know, is eight hours a day. Your perfect amount may be different so I encourage you to figure out what that is. What most don't understand is that there are specific hormones

 that are replaced at different times of the night through a process known as the circadian rhythm. This rhythm affects mental and physical changes throughout your 24 hour day, including the release of key hormones. Some of these hormones help sleep happen while others are reparative in nature. Whatever the case, make sure you're getting enough sleep to maintain healthy cerebral function.

Tip #5 Get Some Fresh Air

Simply getting outside in the fresh air can do wonders to bring your mental clarity. When you partner the fresh air with the exercise, you give yourself a double whammy. The fresh air combined with the deep breathing I spoke about earlier will give your brain the much-needed oxygen.

Tip # 6 Improve Your Attitude

I am sure you've heard it said before that your attitude determines your altitude. Well, your attitude also determines

 your charisma. Have you ever met or seen a charismatic person that had a bad attitude? I never have and I'm sure you haven't either. Here are a few tips that will lead to a better attitude and more charisma.

While there are hundreds of ways you can improve your attitude I am going to give you three quick wins that you can do today.

1) The first is to be aware of what you say to yourself and make sure your self -talk is feeding your mind with only things that will move you forward. If you listen closely to the words you say and the words of those around, you often find that most people are focusing on the negative. Take some time to write down some affirmations by which you tell yourself things you should hear to move forward. A lot of this has to do with reframing how you say things. For instance, you can write down on a 3 x 5 card something like "People enjoy being around me and listening to what I have to say." What a phrase like this does, is it starts to focus

your mind on the type of person you want to be and the associated actions and attitudes that go with it. Along with changing what you say to yourself and becoming aware of what others are saying to you. This leads us to the next step, which is to watch who you hang out with.

2) Have you ever experienced a time when you were around with people and when you left them, you feel down, angry, or negative? On the flip side have you ever been around with people that once you left them you were more energized than when you first arrived in their presence? Who you hang out with and their attitudes can have a direct positive or negative effect on your attitude. Since this is the case, make sure you are surrounding yourself with people that will feed a positive attitude. Both the words you say to yourself and the words other say to you can have an effect on what you focus on. So, this brings us to the third tip on attitude, and that is to focus on solutions and not on problems.

It is very common for people to look at a situation and focus on the problem. We even do this in normal conversation when we say we are good problem solvers. What if instead of being a great problem solver, you are a great solutionist? And yes, solutionist is a real word. You can look it up in the dictionary. Just a slight change in where you focus, from looking at the problem to focusing on the solution, will go a long way to creating a positive attitude. Of course, you must understand the problem, however; the problem should not be the focus of your attention. Adjust your energy from the problem to the solution and you will find that your mind will start to seek out ways to solve your issue.

Tip #7 Be Grateful

There are so many things you can be thankful and grateful for, especially if you have the means and ability to be reading this. Those with charisma are truly grateful for all they have in their life. Take time each day to write down what you are grateful for.

Tip #8 Smile

Your smile can literally change the way you think and also the way others think and act around you. A smile is extremely powerful. Have you ever been walking down the street or in the mall and you saw a young child looking at you with a big smile? As you're reading this you are probably recalling that moment and smiling yourself. A smile is not only powerful, it is also contagious, just like your attitude. Try this little experiment. The next time you are feeling down or in a bad mood, force yourself to smile. Try to smile for at least a minute, but longer if you can. You will find that your attitude will change, even if just a little. Charismatic people use the power of a smile to influence others in a positive way.

Tip #9 Feed Your Brain with Positive Things

The fact that you're reading this book tells me you are the

kind of person that is looking to improve oneself. The books you read or listen to can have a profound effect on your attitude. You can also listen to uplifting music with a positive message, or listen to podcasts through your phone or computer. Give your brain a good dose of positivity every day. This will not only affect your attitude but continuous education will open the door to new opportunities and views to grow your charisma.

Tip #10 Think on Your Feet

This tip is directly in line with decluttering your mind and attitude. You want to train yourself to be quick-witted and be able to have an intelligent conversation. Those with charisma have a certain wit that keeps people engaged. Practice the art of improvisation. There are comedy clubs across the country that have open mic nights or you can take an improv class that many of these clubs offer. Also by feeding your brain, as we discussed in the previous tip, you will make yourself a more well-rounded person and be able to relate to more people on different subjects.

Tip #11 Be More Confident

Don't you just hate when people say be more confident? The question that we all have when we hear that, is, "how"? Well, we've already talked about one way and that is to feed your brain with positive things. This actually is a dual purpose maneuver. Thinking positive releases dopamine - the happy hormone. At the same time, you are able to kill or get rid of negative thoughts. Another way to be more confident is to appreciate who you are and the gifts and skills that you have. This isn't some kind of motivational way of thinking but rather this is really a change in focus. All of us have gifts and if you have any experience in this world, you have developed some skills that you can utilize in different areas of your life. The sooner you understand and know what your gifts and talents are, the better off and more confident you will become. If you don't have many skills, go get one. There are thousands of free courses and videos on YouTube. The biggest thing you will need to do is invest your time.

Okay, so I am going to assume you've gone out and acquired some level of skill. The next step is to see how this skill can be used. This will require a bit of research but find out where your skill is relevant and how it can serve society. Next, I want you to choose one area to focus on, that you found in your research. From here, dive in. Seek to learn everything you can to be the best in this one area. By creating a focus like this, you take your mind off of all the other noises that come your way. Also, as your proficiency grows, so will your confidence. One thing is true and that is, those with charisma have confidence. So, take the steps to create more for yourself.

Tip #12 Be Decisive

Being decisive will do several things for you, the first of which will help with your confidence. When you can make quick decisions, oftentimes, being decisive becomes like any other skill. You get better at it and it increases your ability to make decisions. The other thing that being decisive does is it affects the perception others have of you. When someone sees that you were able to make decisions with authority, not only will they have more respect for you but they will see you as confident and they will see you as someone they can possibly trust. An exercise, similar to the confidence exercise, is you can pick one area of your life where you can be more decisive. The decisions don't need to be big. This can be as simple as being the decision maker on where you are going to go for dinner. You have probably heard or experienced this scenario. "Where do you want to go to eat?" The answer, "I don't know, where do you want to go?" The banter often goes on and on until someone gets tired of the indecision and decides. So the next time someone asks you that question, decide. The series of decisions done over and over again will create and improve your decision-making skills.

Tip #13 Have Empathy

Many people confuse the difference between empathy and sympathy. Sympathy is when you feel bad for somebody or has pity for them. And empathy, on the other hand, is sharing a feeling with somebody else. This can be illustrated while watching a movie. Let's suppose that something happens to a character, something sad. Depending on the relationship that you have built with that character throughout the movie, your response maybe that of slight sadness or if the relationship has developed and you've connected with that character you may even start to cry. This is what is known as an empathetic response.

If you're looking too deep in your relationships you will need to go beyond sympathy. This even goes beyond putting yourself in someone else's shoes. Do you want to gain a deeper understanding and feel how they feel about a particular situation? This is something that a lot of people do mainly because it is not easy. If you will ever take the time to really understand how somebody's feeling, let alone try to feel how they feel. For you, training yourself to have this kind of empathy will really set you apart. By doing this you will be able to relate to the individual and their situation better.

Tip #14 Word Choice

While how you say things are often more important than what you say, the words you choose will affect how the people see you. This is where you want to have a really good understanding of your audience. You'll want to understand their education levels, the type of career they have, and really listen to how they are communicating. And if your education level is high and you are used to using large complicated words and the person you're speaking to, barely graduated high school, the only thing you will accomplish is to have yourself be seen as arrogant and pompous. Not to mention the fact that using this type of verbiage may make the person you're speaking to feel inadequate or bad about themselves. Couple this with the fact that they will not understand what you are trying to say, you will alienate them and fail to connect.

At the same time, if you're dealing with people at a higher education level, for those that use a higher degree of language, you will need to further educate yourself to be able to speak to them with the type of warning they are used to. Depending on your sphere of influence, using higher level language won't typically be necessary. But again, this goes back to knowing your audience and having a bit of background. So as you take the time to develop your language skills for those rare occasions where you may be speaking to a high-level academic, spend more of your time understanding those that you were coming to contact with the most.

Tip #15 Speak Slower

We previously spoke about voice inflection and utilizing the highs and lows in your voice. Speaking slower doesn't mean that you will utilize that monotone expression I spoke of earlier. Those with charisma speak slowly and deliberately to ensure that they are able to get their point across. Yes, they may speak faster in certain situations depending on their audience and you will often see them speeding up and slowing down their speech for emphasis. However, if you listen long enough you will come to hear a speech pattern that is slow and deliberate. This is something charismatic people do on purpose. Have you ever had an experience where somebody is trying to tell you a story and they are so excited about the story, they seem to be bouncing all over the place? While the point of the story may be fantastic but their delivery may have left you wondering or worse, annoyed.

Let's suppose you are engaging with somebody for the first time. And as you're introducing yourself, you are starting to get to know them and you want to make sure that you were able to articulate your answers to questions they may have, in a manner that is slow and deliberate. There is a fine balance though. You don't want to speak so slow that you see there is class over and you lose their attention. Some of this goes much deeper into the study of social psychology. You'll want to understand what their social styles and be able to communicate in their styles. Let me elaborate a little further on social styles.

Social Styles

There are four main social styles that you are coming to contact with. These are the type A or driver style, the expressive, the analytical, and the amiable. Each of the styles communicates differently. Two of them prefer a more intense, possibly passionate, type of discussion while the other two prefer a slower and softer tone of voice. In this section, I will be speaking about the extremes so it's important to understand that you will come into contact with all types in between. Let's understand what the social styles are and how you can relate to them.

The Driver or Type A

This social style is one that you have most likely encountered in your life. These individuals are the type that set goals and don't stop working until the goal is accomplished. They rarely let anything get in their way. They also have a unique way of communicating. When speaking to them, it is very important that you get to the point as quickly as possible because they are most likely on a mission and don't have time to waste sitting around listening to you, dancing around when it's not needed. So, if you want to be able to relate to this social style, make sure you are able to get your point across in as few words as possible.

The Expressive

This social style is often considered as the life of the party. Rarely are they anywhere where they don't know somebody and if they don't know somebody, in a very short time they will introduce themselves and get to know new faces. The Type A manner of speaking does not work for these individuals. The expressive social style likes to engage in conversation. Compared to the Type A, they will use significantly more words than the previous social style may use so, it is important that when you are communicating with them, you understand their need to be heard and engage in active banter.

The Analytical

The analytical is the type of social style that is also very factual like the Type A personality, however, this social style relishes the details. If you are going to engage in a conversation with an analytical social style make sure you don't only have the facts but also accuracy regarding these facts because they will check on it. When you take the time to speak the language of an analytical type, what you will get in return is data and information that is highly detailed, has few to no errors, and you can be certain that they have check their facts not once, not twice, but most likely several times.

The Amiable

The amiable social style is often likened to that of a counselor. This person is a great listener. They take the time to understand and are one of the most adept at being empathetic. What you can learn from the amiable social style is patience. When dealing with them, make sure you consider their understanding nature and respect their time. While they are very patient, showing respect for their opinion and their time will show them that you care. At the end of the day, this social style is one that is known as caring.

At this point, you may be wondering how are you supposed to be all of these people in one and the answer is you don't. The first thing you need to do is understand your own social style. Having a strong awareness of who you are and how you deal with others, is the first step in understanding the other social styles mentioned. The second thing to do is to simply observe. You'll want to observe those around you and see if you can identify, first off, those that have a similar social style to your own. You can do this in any setting where people gather. You can watch conversations, interactions, and look out for the subtle nuances that each social style brings. The reason to start with your own is that you are most familiar with your own way of thinking and so, it is the easiest style to pick out and understand. Once you have mastered your own social style you can add your observations of another social style to the mix.

It is important to remember that most people are not just one type of social style. In fact, most of us are able to maneuver within all four, given the situation and circumstance. However, we do have a dominant type of style that we tend to gravitate toward. As you do your observations, you will notice that you will be able to pick out the social style that most resembles your own. With practice, you will be able to slowly start to recognize all four in any given situation. The important thing to remember is that this will not come without practice. The more often you can practice and the more often you engage with others, the quicker you will be able to grasp a strong foundation in identifying and dealing with each social style.

Chapter 3: The Body

Here you will be given tips as they relate to your physical body. In the mind chapter, we already spoke about confidence, however, confidence doesn't just occur in the mind but there are also physical aspects that create chemical reactions in the body that can lead to greater confidence. In her book, *Presence*, Amy Cuddy speaks about changing your body language to improve your confidence. What her research found was that the way we stand, and the way we sit, as it relates to body position, affects not only how we are perceived but it also affects the hormones that are released in our body. She found that if you stand in the Superman pose for two minutes, testosterone levels increased. She found out that this led to greater confidence from this simple act. So, not only can you increase your confidence from the mental aspect but you could also physically alter the hormones that are released in your body through your body position. Since we are talking about Amy Cuddy's book, this leads us to the next tip which is to increase presence for more charisma.

Tip #16 Increase Your Presence

What is Presence? Presence is not one thing but several aspects that create your overall presence.

Confidence is a big part of presence and we already spoke about few ways that you can increase your confidence. In addition to that, there are a few other actions you can take to increase your presence. One of these is to improve your first impression. When you're meeting someone for the first time, what is that first impression that you make? We spoke a little bit about your body language but there are other things to consider as well. One of them is your handshake. Do you have a dead fish handshake, the overbearing knuckle crushing handshake, or is your handshake firm and given with authority? Whether you realize it or not, your handshake tells people a lot about you or at least that makes them think certain things about you. Another aspect of the first impression is your facial expressions. We already talked about the smile. Not only can this affect how you're thinking but as we discussed, a smile is contagious. Greeting somebody with a smile can influence how they perceive you and your presence around them.

Tip #17 Get in Shape

While it would be nice to think that we are not judged by our appearance, the fact of the matter is that people do judge a book by its cover. I probably don't have to tell you how exercise and eating healthy can lead to more energy. This translates directly to the energy that you give off to those around you. While you don't have to have a perfect body to be charismatic, eating properly and doing a little bit of exercise several days a week will not only affect you physically but it will enhance a lot of the mental strengthening we've already spoken about. Although all the benefits of exercise are widely known, many don't take advantage of this simple implementation. Yes, I know, it's not always easy, as getting to the gym is hard with all the commitments, work, the kids, and the hundreds of other things that go on in our lives. However, since learning about charisma is important to you and I assume it is, or you would not be reading this book, getting in shape is probably one of the simplest things you can do to take yourself to the next level in many areas of your life, not to mention charisma. So take more of those walks that we talked about and replace that soda with water.

Tip #18 What Are You Wearing?

Continuing to talk about how people judge a book by its cover, we need to talk about what you're wearing. What you wear will have a great deal to do with the environment that you're in, obviously. In some environments, it may be appropriate for you to be wearing a three-piece suit while in other, jeans and a polo or T-shirt, is more appropriate. So this isn't about vanity. This is about relatability and standing out, but not too much. People notice different things and often your clothing can be used as a conversation starter. For example, for a man, if he is wearing one of the wood grained style watches that are available today, he may subtly stand out because it is not the normal type of watch someone would see. Meeting someone for the first time, they may say,

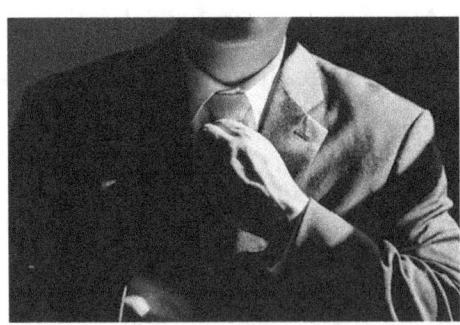

"Nice watch, where did you get it?" Now, your job, if you are wearing an article of clothing or jewelry that you know is a conversation starter, be prepared with

an answer. Show confidence in where you purchased it and be able to speak to some of the details.

There are several great YouTube channels and websites where you can learn some of the basics from men's and women's fashion. You don't have to break the bank, but you do need to look put together. Like we've talked about, you will be judged. Whether that is right or wrong is not the point, the fact remains that this is part of our society and you'll need to take cues and lessons from some of the best-dressed people out there. Just look at some of the people you admire. Next time you are around them, take a look at their clothes. Look at how they are wearing their clothes.

Whatever the dress code is or style you decide to choose, make sure you are wearing the best fitting and best possible clothing for your budget. How something fits is significantly more important than how much something costs. I've seen speakers on stage wearing a T-shirt, jeans, and sneakers and their presence and charisma were greater than other speakers wearing a suit and tie. It was more about how they wore their clothing versus the actual clothing themselves. Now, if you can afford to splurge then go for it. The point is, if you are not already doing so, you need to be conscious of what you are wearing.

Tip #19 Make Eye Contact

When meeting somebody for the first time, a quick way to be thrown back into the shadows is to not make eye contact. Eye contact says a lot about you, such as your confidence and trustworthiness. I'm sure you've met that person before, or maybe it's you, where you meet somebody and as soon as you go to shake their hand, their eyes dart to the floor. Someone with charisma will look you straight in the eye and it won't be that creepy type of flooring stare that makes anybody uncomfortable. They will keep eye contact with you as they're speaking to you and as you reply to them and periodically they will break your gaze but then look back with more eye contact. It is important whether you are speaking to an  individual or to a group, that you make eye contact. In a group, you can bounce from person to person as you're having a conversation to ensure that everyone remains engaged. Either, make sure you are making eye contact to show your charisma.

Tip #20 Be A Mirror

Along with eye contact, try to mirror the other person's body language as you were speaking to them. For instance, if you were both sitting down and they are sitting back in their chair with their legs crossed, you may try to sit in a similar manner. The trick here is to do it subtly. When you mirror somebody it creates a familiarity and builds rapport subconsciously. However, be careful not to do this too much or too overly. Because this tactic has been around for so long many people understand the mirroring technique and may find it annoying if you mirror their every move.

Now you learn some tips and tricks for using your body to become more charismatic. In each of these areas, there is a much deeper study for you to take, so, I encourage you to take the time to pick one or two of the items that are easiest for you to execute today and implement them. At the same time, take one of these tips that you may be unfamiliar with and do a deeper dive to get more familiar with how to take action in that area.

Chapter 4: The Relationship

Now that you've worked on your mind and body it's time to take things to the next level and that is in the development of your relationships. The amount of charisma you have will be directly related to how you deal with other people. This is where the rubber meets the road.

Tip #21 Control Your Voice

There are a few aspects of your voice that affect how you are perceived and are directly correlated to charisma. The first is your voice inflection. When you speak, do you speak in a monotone manner or do you use a combination of highs and lows to emphasize different points? You will notice those with high-level of charisma have a great deal of variety in their voice when they are speaking. You will not hear them sound dull and boring but rather you will hear passion and excitement in what they say. At the same time, even with the use of highs and lows, there is also a sense of calm and control in their voice. For instance, as they relate something tragic to you, they do it from a place of control. The story they are spinning may have pieces that are out of control but as they relay the story they are always in control. You will seldom hear them panic even when they are speaking from a place of urgency. Their communication, while calm, will be no less passionate.

Another aspect of voice is using a series of ums, likes, or well you know. The charismatic person is fluid in their conversation and has the appearance of knowing what they are talking about, even when they don't. Using too many filler words in a conversation gives a sense of low confidence on the topic you are speaking about or a lack of knowledge and understanding. This is something you will need to practice because all of us use words like this without thinking about it. One way to help with this is to pause between thoughts. If you are speaking to someone and you feel the urge to say um, simply pause and say nothing. There may be an awkward silence and you if you get stuck, you can simply say, "Just a minute, I want to make sure I say this just right." Learning this takes practice - a lot of practice. This is especially true if you've developed a history of filling the silent spaces in your conversation with the dreaded ums and uhs.

Tip #22 Be Well- Rounded

One thing you will want to be sure to do is to know a little bit about a lot of different things. Have you ever found someone that is able to speak on the topics that you were interested in and they come across as engaging? Knowing a little bit about a lot of different areas will allow you to establish connectivity and rapport with the individual you're speaking to. If you are going to a party you may want to find out who will be attending and get an understanding of their backgrounds and interests. I am not saying to be that creepy person and stalk them. However, we are in an age where you can easily look people up on social media to get an understanding of some of the things that they are interested in and become more knowledgeable in those areas. For instance, if you know your host is a fan of soccer you may not know the

difference between a dribble and a bicycle kick, but you can take the time to understand what his favorite team is or maybe their favorite player. You can get a general understanding of the game and about the team from hundreds of different websites. This doesn't mean you need to become a soccer expert, but having a basic understanding may be able to allow you to have a conversation that will peak your host's interest.

Apart from studying websites you can take online courses, read books like this, or listen to podcasts. There is so much information out there that you will not be short on trying to find information on any topic you wish. The only issue most people have is they don't take the time to do this. Become curious. Develop an insatiable thirst for knowledge, this way, when someone talks to you about a subject they are interested in, you can have a meaningful conversation with them and develop the type of connection that only those with charisma can.

Tip #23 Be a Good Storyteller

On the heels of being well-rounded, you will also want to improve your storytelling skills. Nothing is more engaging than speaking to somebody who can take you down a path and enlighten your senses with a good story. Let's look at an example, let's suppose you were describing someone going to the market and what happened there. You could say something like:

Suzy got in her car and went to the store. Suzy got some produce to make a salad. She picked up some lettuce, tomatoes, cucumbers, and carrots. After she finished paying for them she was a little agitated because of the long lines. By the time she got home, she was really hungry.

Okay, not too exciting right? There were a couple of things that maybe left you with questions. What if you add a little more detail like this:

After a long frustrating day at the office, Suzy got in her car and went to the store to pick up some produce to make a salad. She had eaten a lot of junk food over the weekend and since this was Monday, she wanted to start the week off healthy. Plus, she had some cooked chicken in the refrigerator so she figured this would go nicely with the delicious healthy salad. The produce section had a vast array of items Suzy could choose from. She was a bit of a picky eater and tended to stick to the same four ingredients. She picked up some lettuce, tomatoes, cucumbers, and carrots. She thought about getting an onion but then thought of how her breath might smell the next morning at work, so she decided against it. She was famished. Her day was so hectic she hadn't taken the time to eat lunch. As she rounded the corner of one of the aisles she saw that every checkout line had at least five people in it and everyone had a full shopping cart. "Did everybody in town decide to come shopping today?" she thought. After she finished paying for her items, Suzy was a little agitated because of the long lines. It probably had nothing to do with long lines and more to do with the fact that she had a bad day and was famished. By the time she got home, she could not wait to devour her dinner.

See the difference? You were able to get a little more detail about the story, Suzy's day, and understand more about her frustration. The second story paints a picture. I could have gone deeper in describing the store, the produce area, the environment, the people there, and so on. The important thing to remember is we are constantly being told stories and we've grown accustomed to and are more engaged when we hear one. Developing this skill of being a good storyteller will not only help you engage those you come in contact with, they will make you better at conveying your message. So take some time to learn this skill and watch the charisma flow out of you.

Tip #24 Listening Skills

Listening skills is probably one of the most underrated and underutilized skills when it comes to communication and building relationships. When engaged in a conversation, many of us are concerned with what we are going to say next as the person we are speaking with shares their point of view. If you can take the time to listen twice as much as you speak, several things will happen. The first thing is, you will learn a lot about the other person when you speak less and listen more and you will be able to gain insight from what the other person to sharing with you. The other thing that will happen is that you may be viewed as a great conversationalist. I know this sounds contrary to conventional wisdom but when you say less and give the other person a chance to share their point of view, they will appreciate the fact that you allow them to hear the most beautiful voice in the world and that is their own voice. Many people value their opinion more than anyone else, therefore, when they are allowed to express those opinions freely, without interruption, their ego will be fed and satisfied. At the same time, this requires much less work for me. Perfectly timed questions here and a comment

 there can keep the conversation flowing. So to improve your charisma, score in their eyes by trying not to impress them with your brilliance but by impressing them with the sound of their voice.

Tip #25 It's Not About You It's About Them

I'd like to add on from the listening skills and speak to the fact that as you speak with and listen to someone, it is very important to remember that they are listening to that all important radio station that we all listen to, WIIFM – What's In It For Me. We spend the majority of our waking hours thinking about us. You might be saying, "No, that's not true, I think about others all the time." While this may be true, from the time you wake up, you are typically thinking about what you have to do that morning and throughout the day. As you engage in conversation, you are thinking about what you're going to say and some of us are worried about what the other person is thinking of us – thoughts like "Are my clothes right? Does my hair look good? What if they don't like me?" If we are thinking these things, just imagine what the other person is thinking about. Most likely they are having similar thoughts. If you can understand this, this will put you at an advantage and give you the ability to shape the conversation in such a way, like we spoke about in the previous section, that the person is feeling heard. Our egos are fragile and if you can remember, that it's not about you it's about them, your charisma will be taken to new level.

Tip#26 The Power of Appreciation

If you were to survey a large group of people you would find out, especially in the workplace, that they don't feel appreciated. When you are engaged in a conversation and you either compliment them or show appreciation for something they are either saying or maybe wearing, you will stand out from the crowd. This is not to say that the appreciation is to be false or shallow. Your compliment needs to be genuine. Most of us, including yourself, know when someone is feeding us a line or showing us appreciation just to get something from you. So, if you meet someone and you truly can't find anything to show appreciation for, it is better to say nothing at all than to fake interest and admiration. At the same time, as I stated before, we all have unique gifts so it shouldn't be too difficult to find something about the other person that you can appreciate or provide a compliment.

Tip #27 Be Relatable

As humans, we tend to be most comfortable with what is familiar to us. Just like with appreciation, this is not something you do without being genuine. If somebody is sharing a story and you've had a similar experience, or know someone with a similar experience, share those experiences with that person you are engaged with. You don't need to have an elaborate story or something that will "one up them". You just need to show them that you understand and can relate to their experience. Remember, people don't need you to impress them. The fact of the matter is they may be trying to impress you. All they want to know is if there is a common ground where you both can meet. Being relatable can take you a long way to developing the charisma you desire.

What's next? It's time to put all of this knowledge to work. It's time to show you how these tips can be implemented and put into action.

Chapter 5: Putting It All Together

A lot of the tips we've talked about will cross over and complement each other, but how do you put them all together so you are progressing toward gaining more charisma? I'm glad you asked. Let's walk down this road together and see what all of this looks like.

All of this boils down to awareness, awareness of yourself, your thoughts, how you dress, and how you hold yourself. After you, the next phase of awareness is your surroundings. Become acutely aware of what is happening around you, both while you are engaged with someone and when you are surveying the room.

Here is the scenario:

Your boss has invited you to a conference in order to network with other people from your industry. You aren't very social so all these thoughts start racing through your head. "Why did he invite me? I don't know what to say? What am I supposed to do at these conferences?" The questions and noise continue to fire away in your head. STOP!

Your mind is cluttered, so time to declutter. One of the tips we talked about to help declutter your mind is to write things down. Journal what you are feeling and become aware of these questions you are asking yourself. Some may be relevant and some may be a response to fear. Write down the answers to your relevant questions and begin to understand the answers.

Be grateful for the opportunity and understand that your boss would not be spending the money to fly you to a conference if she did not feel you have something to offer. Did I tell you that the conference is being held in Orlando at the Disney Resort? Did you catch what happened? By shifting your thinking, you are reframing and improving your attitude. Now it's time to prepare. After all, you want to make sure you understand who you will be coming in contact with and you'll want to be well rounded to be able to engage in a meaningful conversation. You've been given two weeks to prepare, so you have plenty of time for some research.

Next on your agenda is to make sure you understand the dress code. You may need to purchase few items if you don't already have what is appropriate. Like we talked about, you don't need to get the most expensive things. You just need to make sure what you have to fit well. Instead of shopping, you may need to go to a tailor. Depending on the town you live in, you should have plenty of time if you're doing this immediately.

Okay, it's time to get to the conference. Wow, that was a fast two weeks, right? You have clothes that fit you well, you've done your research on who will be there, the topics that will be discussed, and some of the key players your boss is interested in meeting. Once you arrive at the hotel and check-in, it's time for the first social gathering. Again, thoughts start to swirl in your head, but you're prepared. You take a few minutes to write down what you're feeling, what you plan to do, and maybe look at a few of the affirmation cards you previously wrote, after reading about it in Tip #3. You're well rested because you know part of having charisma is getting enough sleep and you decide to take a quick walk outside to clear your head and get some fresh air.

Okay, it's time to mingle. The first person you come in contact with is Steven. He is someone your boss wants to do business with and you know he's an avid tennis player like yourself. You introduce yourself and exchange friendly banter. You then mention the weather and say how this is a perfect tennis weather. You see his eyes light up. "You play tennis?" he asks. "Yes, I do!" you respond with enthusiasm and a smile. You then begin to ask him about tennis, how he got started, how often he plays and so on. You maintain good eye contact and you make sure you are utilizing your highs and lows in your voice as the conversation continues. You show him appreciation as a fellow tennis player and can relate to a lot of what he goes through since he plays tournaments just like you.

As your conversation continues you continue to keep the conversation focused on him while added your input here and there. You are able to share stories about your playing history and how much enjoyment you get out of the game. Both of you are relating to each other and your confidence is showing. The conversation turns from tennis to business and he appears to be interested in what you have to say. Understanding where this conversation has gone, you are excited. However, you remember to speak slowly and make sure you are, again, utilizing your voice but not so much that you stumble over words.

Throughout the conference, you are able to meet several people and have similar conversations. On the flight home, your boss tells you that Steven was very complimentary of you and how much charismatic you were. Because of your connection to him, he is interested in doing business with your company and that definitely bodes well for you and your career.

In this brief story, can you see how many of the tips we covered came into play? Most of what you learned worked together and complement each other and together, they make you charismatic.

Conclusion

Thank you for making it through to the end of this book, let's hope it was informative and able to provide you with all of the tools you need to achieve your goals, whatever they may be.

The next step is to apply what you've learned in the real world. I suggest you try not to tackle all the tips at once. There are simply too many to apply at the same time.

Start with one or two of your favorites. Practice them over a week's time. After that, add another tip and then one to two each week. As you add new skills to your arsenal grows, continue to work on the previous weeks' skills. Over time you will start to notice a difference in your interactions and how you feel about yourself. The key is to take a methodical and step by step approach in the application of these steps. Okay, I almost forgot the most important part. You MUST, and I repeat, you MUST, practice this in and around other people. The only way you will be able to sharpen your skills is by practicing everything you've learned while interacting with others. Make sure to practice this with people you know and with strangers. I say this because some of you will be tempted to practice in a vacuum. I cannot emphasize enough the importance of applying what you've learned. You will see the fastest result this way.

Finally, if you found this book useful in any way, a review on Amazon is always appreciated!

www.ingramcontent.com/pod-product-compliance
Lightning Source LLC
Chambersburg PA
CBHW050025230526
45470CB00003B/1135